To Kathy
With good wishes,
Van Parker

Letting in the Light

New and Selected Poems

Van Parker

BALBOA.
PRESS

A DIVISION OF HAY HOUSE

Balboa Press books may be ordered through booksellers or by contacting:

Balboa Press
A Division of Hay House
1663 Liberty Drive
Bloomington, IN 47403
www.balboapress.com
1 (877) 407-4847

Because of the dynamic nature of the Internet, any web addresses or links contained in this book may have changed since publication and may no longer be valid. The views expressed in this work are solely those of the author and do not necessarily reflect the views of the publisher, and the publisher hereby disclaims any responsibility for them.

The author of this book does not dispense medical advice or prescribe the use of any technique as a form of treatment for physical, emotional, or medical problems without the advice of a physician, either directly or indirectly. The intent of the author is only to offer information of a general nature to help you in your quest for emotional and spiritual well-being. In the event you use any of the information in this book for yourself, which is your constitutional right, the author and the publisher assume no responsibility for your actions.

Any people depicted in stock imagery provided by Thinkstock are models, and such images are being used for illustrative purposes only. Certain stock imagery © Thinkstock.

Print information available on the last page.

ISBN: 978-1-5043-6225-2 (sc)
ISBN: 978-1-5043-6226-9 (e)

Balboa Press rev. date: 08/01/2016

FOR

My wife, *Lucille (Lucy)*
Our children:
Susan, Beth and Doug
Their spouses:
George and Kim
Our grandchildren:
Grace, Luke and Jamie Murnaghan;
Maddie, Jackson and Faith Parker.

With love and gratitude

Acknowledgements

I would like to express my thanks to:

Bruce Bidwell and Gretchen Skelley
for helping me choose the selected poems.

Lowell Fewster, for the picture on the back cover.

Henry Millan, for suggesting the title.

The helpful, creative people at Balboa Press.

A variety of poets who, without knowing it,
have been my teachers.

Friends, whose encouragement always seems
to arrive at the right time.

Contents

PART 2 - SILENT MUSIC

PART 3 - ROUNDING THIRD

Preface

Writing poems is something I stumbled into late in life. After retiring from the ministry, I started writing observations on various matters in *"The North Star Monthly"* of Danville, Vermont. This evolved into a newsletter sent out to friends and friends of friends. In late 2009 at the age of eighty I began writing poems. That seemed like both a natural next step and the beginning of a new adventure.

Poems tend to start from some place close by - a tree, your next-door neighbor, a flock of geese - and lead us toward wonder and mystery. Billy Collins says he hopes his poems "begin in Kansas and end in Oz." There is something about poetry that refuses to be corralled or tied up in a package.

When writing a poem I am often surprised by the way it comes out. Apparently this is a common experience. Robert Frost said "no surprise for the writer, no surprise for the reader."

Lately it's become clear to me that poetry can reveal connections to parts of ourselves, other people, the earth and what Alcoholics Anonymous calls a Higher Power. Some have said the greatest sickness human beings experience is homesickness. Poetry can't solve every ill but it can, often unexpectedly, indicate a way home.

"Letting in the Light" is my third book of poetry. It's a mixture of poems written over the last six years in a roughly 60/40 ratio of unpublished and published. Having discovered that poems like to speak for themselves, I wish them good travels and Godspeed as they set out on their way. It's been good for me to write them. I hope you will find some resonance as you read them.

Van Parker

How To Be A Poet

(to remind myself)

……..Accept what comes from silence.
Make the best you can of it.
Of the little words that come
out of the silence, like prayers
prayed back to the one who prays,
make a poem that does not disturb
the silence from which it came.

Wendell Berry

Let us return to ourselves and become wholly ourselves. Let us
maintain a half smile on our faces.

Thich Nhat Hanh

PART 1

Grounded

Stop

Sometimes,
when you wake up in the morning,
the most important thing is to stop,

which is possible
even while you are delivering
your neighbor's paper.

Let the motor within you rest
for a while.
Don't rev it up with all the things
you have to do.

Stop,
so you can look and listen.
Watch the birds flying
between the trees in your back yard.

Don't try to accomplish anything,
unless you consider making coffee
an accomplishment.

God already knows you're imperfect
and doesn't need to be informed
of that fact.

Stop long enough to say thanks.

Be Good To Your Mother

If the earth is our mother,
then we're related.

So why in the world
would we want to mistreat her
when we're only hurting ourselves?

She could be telling our species
something we need to hear –

that greed and hunger for power
have gone to our heads,
causing the oceans to rise

and the climate to change
in an odd and unsettling manner.

Better to pay attention
to her cry for help and make amends
by changing our habits,

enlisting the sun and the wind.
and, if you're a poet

who likes to scribble down notes
on a notepad,
using both sides of the paper.

Catch Basin

It seemed fitting
to start a new year
with a new notebook

to write down thoughts
which may or may not
turn into poems.

I think of it as a catch basin,
gathering objects
as they fly by,

stalling them for a while,
waiting to hear
what they have to say

before they run off to
some undisclosed location.

Turning

When something or someone begins to turn
in a new direction, it's easy to miss

because mostly it happens below the surface,
in the dark, unseen until, without giving notice,

it makes itself known. As it did toward
the end of February with two feet of snow

still on the ground. But the air felt different
that day - softer, more of the earth.

Something too good to be true, both gentle and
powerful, serious but light-hearted, was at work,

thawing out what seemed forever frozen in place.
Some call it grace.

Meditation On Melting Snow

Some people say that, when you are meditating,
it helps to have something to meditate on.

So, on a walk in the middle of March, I decided
to meditate on melting snow,
since there was so much of it around,

the piles by the sides of the road slowly shrinking
and forming puddles on the sidewalk.
I wondered "Where is all that snow going?"

Some of it straight into the ground, of course,
some disappearing into the air.
some running into drains.

It would be fun to flow along with a shovelful
or two of this melting snow. Might even take you
somewhere you've always wanted to go.

Relocating

When it's time to leave our home
in Hartmeadow Village
after residing there for 20 years,

it will be with more than a little nostalgia
and best wishes to the neighbors, only one
of whom was there when we arrived

at cottage "I",
a cottage with 13 brother and sister cottages
gathered under the protective wing of a church,

reminding me of a hen sitting above her brood
looking pleased with her 14 offspring
as none of them have caused her any grief
or threatened to run away.

Reasonable Request

The retirement village
we now call home
is a welcoming place.

There's no shortage of things to do
or not do.

You need to pick and choose
among its many offerings

including two exercise groups,
one while sitting, the other while standing-

hiking, canoeing on a nearby river and
walking around the pond –

musicals, festivals and other
similar occasions –

informative lectures, poetry readings,
discussions of current events, trips here
and there. I don't know where to stop.

You can come and go as you please.
Just tell the woman at the desk how many days
or weeks you'll be away.

But *please* push the green button when you
wake up in the morning.
It lets people know you haven't died overnight.

Breaking News From The Pond

There's a pond at Covenant Village.
Four times around it is a mile.
People in the Village and neighboring houses
like to walk there.

It's a stopover for 40-50 Canadian Geese.
Two days ago it looked like the geese
had left for the winter.
Today they're back,
mostly drifting around on the surface,
apparently in no hurry
to return to their winter home.

The only other inhabitant I saw
was a duck, all by itself.
One day the duck was dipping its head
in and out of the pond. No geese in sight.
Two days later it was up on the bank,
cleaning its feathers,
not far from the geese, but still seeming alone.

Cane Country

Graduating to a cane surprised me.
Never thought it would happen.

When my doctor suggested getting
a cane, it seemed like an odd thought

to be revisited at some vague future date.
But being in a community where

any number of canes can be found,
it doesn't look out of place to use one.

Canes offer support, which can keep a person
from leaning too far to the left or the right

or tripping over small obstacles
like roots or uneven sidewalks.

As a class canes can be trusted, since their
reason for being is not to let you down.

Heartwarming Sight

It's a welcome sight when you see people
who like their work

as does the woman who leads exercise classes
on Monday, Wednesday and Friday

at our new home. She looks happy to be there
as she greets elderly exercisers, helping them

get into the rhythm of stretching and bending,
leaning to the left and to the right,

reaching down to the floor and over their heads,
catching on to the cadence

of breathing out and breathing in
while she counts up – 1 - 2 - 3 - 4 - 5

and down - 5 - 4 - 3 - 2 - 1

It makes you aware you've gone somewhere
and done something

as you arrive, more alive,
at the same place you started

Name Tags

Our new home provides its
400 residents with name tags.

Being magnetic, the name tags
easily attach themselves to

a shirt or a sweater,
making it easier

to connect names and faces
so that, when walking down the hall,

going to exercise classes
or picking up the mail

you can say "hello" to Angela
or Harry, or Frank or Mary.

knowing you're calling them
by the right name.

If your name tag gets lost
or mysteriously vanishes,

the management may, on occasion,
declare a name tag amnesty

and provide a replacement
at a much reduced rate.

April Snow

While walking around the pond
on an early April day,

I stopped to talk to a woman
who seemed to have

a good eye for the weather.
She looked in one direction,

noting the color and shape
of the clouds and then in another

toward a patch of blue sky,
offering her opinion that the forecasters

predicting snow tomorrow were probably
right. No sign of ducks or geese

on the pond. Perhaps they had been
advised to stay away a little longer.

An Invitation

Just past the middle of April.
The countryside is waking up.
It's a little greener than yesterday.

Puddles of water by the roadside
with skunk cabbage growing around
them. The temperature close to

seventy degrees Fahrenheit.
The Connecticut shore opening ahead
with Long Island off in the distance.

Clear sky, light breeze, a man tending
bulbs and flowers outside the main
entrance of a place called Mercy Center.

Driftwood gathered in a neat pile.
Two or three people
walking along the beach.

Nothing forced. No artificial ingredients
in the mix. A reminder of what some
have called an Original Blessing.

Waking Up

This morning I woke up laughing.
Not out loud, as it would have disturbed
my wife who was still sleeping.

Can't tell you what I was laughing about.
as I groggily poured water onto the counter,
missing the coffee maker

and remembered old adages such as

"don't make mountains out of molehills" and

"don't cross bridges until you come to them"

which seemed like answers to prayer.

No feelings last forever and this case is no exception.
But, for a short time on an early morning in June
in the northeastern part of Vermont,
there wasn't a cloud in the sky.

Story Of A Clothesline

The clothesline at 3751 Tampico Road
runs from the back of the house
to an old crabapple tree,

a tree which should have died a long time ago.
It's been struck by lightning
and wired together by a previous owner.

The inside is mostly hollow
but each year it produces a crop of crabapples.

My temporary summer assignment
has been to hang out the wash
while the clothes dryer is out of commission.

It's a satisfying job on a warm July day.
Can't see any downside to it,
except some day that old crabapple tree will

fall down and it will be the end of that clothesline
which will have no place to go.

Ode To Some Blueberry Bushes

Recently I've had several conversations
with the 15 blueberry bushes in our back yard.

Not long conversations -
On my part mostly a matter of saying
"Thanks."
Their response being "You're welcome. We've done
the best we can."

"The best" being 81 quarts of berries –

Enough for

blueberry pies
blueberry pancakes
blueberry muffins
blueberries on cereal and ice cream
blueberries by themselves

Enough to freeze
Enough to give to the neighbors

Now just a few berries are left on the bushes,
whose leaves will soon turn red
and drop to the ground

as though those bushes were saying
"We'll be back but we need a rest!"

On Hold

This year fall has been slow to arrive
in northeastern Vermont.

The bright red leaves
on the tree across the valley
have yet to come down and
the grass in the field
is a mid-summer green.

It won't last forever.
Winter will arrive sooner or later.
But it felt like nature itself
had taken a deep breath
as I watched a dozen wild turkeys
stroll through our back yard,

pecking at seeds, insects or whatever
it is wild turkeys eat.
They didn't seem worried that
turkey hunting season was soon to begin.
It was almost enough
to turn me into a vegetarian.

Welcomed

Arriving in North Danville, I noticed the vegetable garden
was covered with a foot and a half of snow -

The man who looks after the house when we're away
had plowed a path to the front door –

A neighbor left some firewood, neatly arranged on the porch
and, with it, a Christmas tree -

Our daughter, who lives one town away, came over with her
three legged dog and cooked the supper.

Turned on the news, then turned it off,
thankful that someone had turned up the heat.

Christmas Eve

Today I scrapped a poem
It wasn't going anywhere
It was a relief
to get rid of it

Besides, it's Christmas Eve
in Danville Vermont,
where our family has gathered
for the last 20 years

It's a time to catch up,
tell stories, drink hot chocolate,
eat lasagna, check on the weather
at nearby ski areas

and go to church where we'll
be reminded that, in spite of
the terrible things we do to
each other and to mother earth,

God hasn't given up on us
and signs of kindness and good
will show up everywhere
as in that Bethlehem stable

Then, at the end of the service,
we'll light candles,
sing Silent Night
and go home

Looking For A Car

Buying a new used car
is an interesting process
when the buyers are 86 and 84

and one has stopped driving.
You tend to approach this matter
from a different perspective,

seeking counsel from relatives
and friends with the thought that
one or both of you

might outlive the car,
which prompts questions
to car dealers such as:

"How long before the gaskets
start leaking oil?"

"Will the heating system work
for several more years?"

"What about the brakes?"

A good mechanic can answer
such questions. But no one can
guarantee how long anything

or anyone can last and it's
probably a waste of time to ask.

Takes A While

A man from the maintenance staff
at the Village just came by
in response to my wife's request

to check on the water heater.
After a brief inspection he advised me,
before starting the washer,

to turn on the hot water faucet in the sink
and let it run until the water becomes
hot. It takes a while for

the hot water to circulate through
the pipes he explained
before going on his way –

which reminded me that it takes
quite a while for the glue to dry
on a chair you may be fixing.

It takes at least a week
for a seed to germinate after
being set in the ground

and it often takes us a long time
to discover the simplest,
most accessible things.

Hidden Treasure

Emily Dickinson, I've been told,
wrote over 1,700 poems, none of which
were entered in a poetry contest

or ranked and rated by a panel of
judges. Apparently she left these poems
around the house in Amherst where

she lived her whole life and where
they were stranded until after Emily died
and somebody rescued them and sent them

on their way. One cannot help but feel
that Emily would be proud of them. She
put so much effort into raising them.

This shy and reclusive poet, who never
gave birth to a girl or a boy, and only rarely
left her house, raised these 1,700 poems

to be a credit to her parenting. They
have worked hard, gone many places and,
if some of them are a bit tired,

they deserve a rest. But I would guess
that most of them will keep on working.

An Ode To Caption Phones

They're called caption phones
because they put words on a screen
so that people who can't hear the words
can see them.

Caption phones require both speakers
and listeners to slow down.
It takes a few seconds for the words
to get printed -

providing verbal speed bumps,
making listeners appear either thoughtful
or slow- witted.

Caption phones invite you to take a deep breath
while they send messages like
"pay attention" and "what's your hurry?"

A Visit

A President and a Pope,
one coming with his family
to greet the other at the airport.

A feeling of anticipation, the
possibility that what has always been
doesn't have to always be.

News commentators smiling,
as though overtaken
by a spirit they couldn't explain,

hearing a plea and a challenge
to take care of our home
because it belongs to all

and to welcome the stranger
in our midst because we have
been immigrants and strangers.

Children, all along the route,
looking happy. A little girl
with a plea that her father

not be sent back to
where he came from.
The poorest, the most needy

front and center.
Everyone included.
A glimpse of who we are

and who we are meant to be.

Natural Mix

Is it possible
or even desirable
to have your feet on the ground
and your head in the clouds

at the same time?
It makes an odd picture
when you think about it
or attempt to paint it.

But there's enough evidence
to conclude
that the down to earth and the holy
are a natural mix

as we thank God for daily bread
and for water and fresh air,
for sunsets and sunrises
and rainbows and other surprises

and conclude for ourselves
that the holy and the earthy
cannot be split,
one from the other..

Infection

It seemed to emerge
from some deep place –
people saying they wanted

to help refugees find
a new home.
Women and men

of all religious persuasions
or none they can name
moved by the sight

of the body of a 3 year old boy
washed up on a beach
or sharing a common memory

of being outsiders and
having no one to
take them in.

A quiet power spreading
from person to person
like a good kind of infection,

A sense of what Robert Frost
meant when he said "Something
there is that doesn't love a wall."

Polishing Silver

Among other recent discoveries,
I've found the satisfaction
of polishing silver, including:

a dozen spoons over 100 years old
a plate
a tray
2 or 3 items I can't describe

Feels like you've accomplished something
when you polish silver
and it begins to shine again

just like it did
a long time ago

No Complaints

(For Earl Sanderson on his 89th birthday)

Earl keeps going.
He lives by himself
since his wife died a decade ago.

It's a comfortable house
and he knows where everything is.
He hopes, with a little help,
to stay there the rest of his life.

His daughter brings in dishes
he can heat up for a meal and
organizes his pills on the kitchen table.
His son mows the lawn in the summer
and clears the snow in the winter.

A well-read man, these days
Earl listens to talking books
since he can no longer read the print.

Earl's not an anxious person.
He lives in the present, appreciates the past.
He's always glad to see folks who
come by for a visit.

Earl never complains.
No point in it. No need for it.
He counts his blessings.
Earl's cup is more than half full.
It overflows!

Vacancy

A few days ago
our neighbor, Cathy, died.
She was more than a decade
younger than either of us.

She came to Hartmeadow
about 10 years ago.
Now it's hard to imagine
the place without her.

She would remind us if
we'd left a car window open
or forgotten to turn off
the lights in the car.

When we were gone for the summer,
she'd tell us the news
of our neighbors.

She celebrated every birthday
and holiday and loved to pass out
candy on any occasion.

She had a way of seeing what mattered
and a twinkle in her eye that
nothing could put out.

On the day Cathy died
the automatic timer turned
the lights back on in her house.

Haven

(a dog recollected)

We found him at Dog Haven
where he was the dog of the week.
His name was Homer. It seemed to fit,
so we didn't change it.

A medium sized brown and white dog
of no particular breed, Homer
looked scared and shaky. Give him time
and he'll be fine

the woman at Dog Haven said.
She was right about that. Of the four dogs
we'd owned, Homer turned out
to be the best.

On a walk he'd stay with you,
didn't need a leash. If he wanted
to get in or out of the house, he'd bark once
then wait for someone

to open the door. Homer liked to be warm.
In the winter he'd lie by the fireplace
with Louie, our cat,
the cat's head cradled in his mouth.

That last winter Homer looked peeked.
On an early spring day he died
in front of a space heater that
wasn't plugged in.

Initials

One of the two "eating out" groups
to which I belong consists of retired
male ministers and calls itself the G.O.P.

which has nothing to do with political leanings
and stands for "Grumpy Old Preachers",

though none of them are grumpy and
most have stopped preaching.

But, since they range from slightly past 70 to
quite close to 90, the "old" part applies.

One wonders whether the name of the group
should be changed, but it doesn't seem

necessary since the members already know
who they are and who they are not.

Succession

It's become clear to me
that one of the best things
older people can do
is step aside.

That doesn't mean vanishing
or hiding out somewhere.
Just don't block the way
for your successors.

It's time to listen more
and talk less, to cheer on
the next generation
and the one after it.

Don't think of yourself
as a has-been but as a link
in a chain, or a bridge,
or something like that.

PART 2

Silent Music

Letting In The Light

Keep the door open,
along with a window or two.

It circulates the air
as you go about

doing the things
you always do –

like walking the dog,
saying "hi" to a neighbor.

No need to be clever
or to impress anyone.

Just keep the door open.
Allow some light to shine through.

Unexpected

When no way looks open

and all the exits seem blocked

When you don't know where to turn

it may be the right time

for real learning to start

When you can't do what you used to

and the list of losses is long and boring,

it could lead to the discovery

that the gains have

exceeded the losses

Short Cut

In human beings
the head and the heart
are not far apart.

It's only a foot or so
from one to
the other.

But the connections
between the two
often get blocked

by varying kinds
of debris, which
may be why poetry

can help clear the way,
providing a short cut
from one to the other.

Silences

Silence comes in many varieties-

Stony Silence:

Not speaking to each other

Awkward Silence:

Not knowing what to say

Companionable Silence:

Not needing to say anything

Pregnant Silence:

Giving birth to a new way of saying
what you want to say

Silent Music

Couldn't help but feel
the silence
when I turned off the TV
last night.
It was a restful silence.

It didn't give any notice
of its arrival.
It was just there
like an old friend
who happened by.

A long time ago
I read a book called
"Silent Music."
It was something like that -
a kind of harmony.

It offered no advice,
had no agenda.
It didn't say anything
or solve any matters. It
made everything look different.

No Rush

Sunday, the longest day of the year,
started out rainy and ended sunny,
living up to its name

The bus at Covenant Village
made its rounds, taking people to churches
and back home

Robins came out
from wherever they were hiding
to patrol the lawn

Even though we missed church,
it felt like a Sabbath
as I flattened some packing boxes
and took them down the hall
to be recycled
and as someone at our lunch table
started the meal with a prayer.

Pictures

There are three pictures
on the walls of our living room
taken by a photographer friend.

One is a Cuban woman who
I would guess is in her thirties.

Another shows a Guatemalan boy
of about twelve, sitting on a step.

In the third three older men appear
to be thoughtfully conversing.

One can only guess what's on the
minds of the people in the pictures.

Has the woman just heard something
she can hardly believe?

Might the boy be dreaming about
things he can't yet put into words?

Could the three men be discussing the
news of their Guatemalan village?

Has the photographer revealed
something of the face of God
etched into those five faces?

Occasional Visitor

Poems don't exactly
fly through the air
but from time to time
one may land on your shoulder

and, in a tentative way,
announce its presence
Then it becomes a matter
of deciding

what to do with it
But poems like to speak for
themselves, so the chances
are you don't need to do

anything except pay attention
and let it have its say
before it flies away to
wherever it came from
or wherever it's going

About Angels

Angels, sometimes defined as God's messengers,
are hard to spot.

You can't tell at a glance whether they are
or are not.

They don't sprout wings or wear nametags
or look different from others around them.

Only a few have celestial voices
and some sing off key.

But one thing you can say about them
is that they show up when least expected

with a smile or a dish or a prescription
you didn't even know you needed.

Whoa!

Time goes by quickly
when you get older.
That's what I've been told.

Now here I am adding
my testimony to others
that in the latter stages of life

time picks up speed. Some may
disagree with this thought
and hold that time goes on

at the same steady pace
it always has.
I respect their opinion.

But, if this is the case, why
is it that the weekly intervals
between filling my pill box

get shorter and shorter,
making a week ago feel like
the day before yesterday?

Summing It Up

Having already reached the age of 86
I'd like to share a few thoughts
on my eventual demise.

It would be nice if the cause of death
could be listed as "extreme laziness"
or by a line which read

"He gradually wore out,
died in a timely manner
and wasn't mad at anybody."

Obviously we don't have control
over the time and place
of our departure from this earth.

But at least you can express
your preferences,
which I just did.

Regret

Except as a small boy
I can't recall hugging my Dad
or telling him I loved him

I wish I had
It would have meant a lot to him
and to me but I didn't know that then

I often hugged my Mother
It seemed the natural
thing to do

The day I left New England
at age 24, for my first congregation
in southern Ohio

Dad said something like
"If you get sleepy, pull off the road"
I looked at him and noticed

that there were tears in his eyes
We shook hands and I said
"thanks" and "good-bye"

Longevity

Please don't tell me about your grandmother
who lived to be 104
and drove to church and the grocery store
until she was 101 and a half

or what a remarkable specimen
was great uncle Charlie
who died at the age of 99,
shortly after chopping a cord of wood.

I'll settle for 85, a good allotment,
plus whatever more time may remain

to say outrageous things,
thank God for more than can be said
and stay out of the way.

Easter Service

At the beginning
of the Easter service

the minister said this year it
felt more like Good Friday

since Easter followed so closely
the bombing of the railroad station

and the airport in Brussels, Belgium.
As she and a lay leader lit candles

in memory of those who were killed,
there was no denying the pain and the loss.

Still, the old familiar words "Christ is risen"
were said again and somehow took hold.

You could feel it during the "Halleluiah Chorus"
and as people greeted each other after the service.

Riding home through the country, it seemed like
every yard had its quota of newly arrived daffodils.

Peaceful Haircut

On a recent trip to the barber's I noticed a mother
had brought her two sons to get a haircut.

The boys are two years apart the mother said,
the older one five, the younger one three.

Judging by their dress and haircuts,
I concluded they were Orthodox Jews.

The father, apparently a Rabbi, came by
and checked his older son's haircut,

offering a suggestion to the barber.
Being midweek it wasn't anybody's Sabbath

but, as I settled into the barber's chair, it seemed
like that family had left a quiet place behind.

I almost went to sleep.

The Gift Of Fresh Air

When giving thanks in your prayers
for God's many gifts,

it's hard to overestimate the value
of the gift of fresh air

If you were to put a price on it,
how much would you charge?

It can't be regulated but keeps
popping up in unsuspected locations,

as in an innocent comment by a child
that makes everyone laugh

It has a way of cutting through fog
and pointing out pretensions

It tells us the emperor has no clothes
and what had seemed like strength

was mostly hot air

Incomplete

One of the grades
some teachers have been known to give
is "incomplete."

It isn't a letter grade like A B or D
or a number such as 73 -,
just "incomplete" -

which isn't a bad way to describe
anyone who is still learning,
whatever the subject may be –

leaving doors open
for discoveries, surprises,
and unexpected breezes –

arriving at the right time
from...... almost anywhere

Indirectly

Sometimes it helps to let go
of a problem or a situation

Don't try to fix it, resolve it,
conquer it. Don't do anything
with it

Approach it from an angle
instead of head on. Just take
note of it

When you can't see very clearly,
instead of charging through the
mist and the fog,

do something that appears
to be unrelated -

watch a game

water a plant

talk to a neighbor
about this or that

Then wait for the skies to clear
See if something begins to emerge,
like an answer to prayer.

Here And Now

Philosophers remind us
that we're meant to live
in the present –
what some call "the now"

So it's better to be
here when you're here
and there when you're there

than it is to be there
when you're here and
here when you're there

I don't know quite what that
means but I think
it makes sense

Lighthearted

There's something light-hearted
at large in the world, making you
laugh or at least smile

Sometimes it arrives like
an uninvited guest
who becomes the life of the party

It's as though,
while you were struggling through
a difficult time

with no solutions in sight,
a neighbor's dog,
most likely a retriever,

came bounding out of the water
and shook himself,
spraying everyone around

and wagging his tail --
a sign of a playfulness
at the heart of everything

Introductions

(loving your neighbor as yourself)

Since it is hard to imagine
a human being
without taking his or her
relationships into account,

the best thing other people
can do for you
might be to help you
get better acquainted with yourself

by pointing out things they see in you
that you didn't know were there -
such as the ability to......
paint a picture
build a house
solve a problem

and then try to return the favor
so that you and your neighbor,
the next time either one of you
looks in the mirror, can say

"I'm glad to meet you!"
"Where have you been?"

Sense Of Humor

A sense of humor
cannot be programmed.
It might show up, uninvited,
at the oddest times

such as at the end of a day
when everything that could go wrong
did go wrong.

It could appear crashing a party
or visit a solemn assembly,
embarrassing you, forcing you

to suppress a smile.
No one can own it or manage it.
It comes in a million varieties,
and seems to know things we don't,

at least in our conscious minds.
It's irreverent in a reverent sort of way
It has a playful quality
as it goes about its business

of dissolving barriers
and reminding people
not to take themselves too seriously.

Life Begins At 36

Don't take that literally.
I just said it to get your attention.
Pick your own dates and times
when you saw something you'd missed

and wondered "Why didn't I see that before?"
Or you heard a knock on the door
which seemed easy to ignore
except it kept coming back,

appearing in a thousand guises –
greeting you in an unexpected rainbow
and in a neighbor
bringing a casserole.

Someone looking for you
when you didn't know you were lost
and, with a smile,
welcoming you home.

It's About Jesus

Christmas doesn't force itself,
demanding your attention, saying
"Here I am!"

It steals into our midst
in music, lights, silence and
through unexpected acts of kindness.

It's angels reassuring
some frightened shepherds
a long time ago.

It's other angels. Perhaps you can
name some, showing up when most needed,
bringing the same message –

"Don't be afraid"

It's a baby named Jesus
bringing God closer, inviting us,
whoever we are, to come in.

Knowing

How can you know and not know
at the same time?
It doesn't make sense.
Either you know something or you don't,
like the answers to questions at a quiz show.

But that's the left side of your brain talking,
the side that demands answers.
Give it credit.
It fixes cars, builds bridges, finds cures for diseases.

But sometimes that side of your brain
forgets its limits, as it attempts to mend
a broken heart or fill an empty space.

Better to pay attention to nudges, inklings,
hints of something unexpected, a kind of knowing,
arriving in its own time, clearing the way ahead.

If

If, in the normal course of your day,
you happen to see someone
sitting in a comfortable chair,
staring out the window
or taking a nap,
don't conclude too quickly
that he or she is wasting time.

It could be they are

-meditating on a situation

-watching birds at the feeder or

- catching up on lost sleep while

reminding themselves to slow down,
and pay attention to a quiet voice
that's never been far off
but often forgotten

Management

It looks like the best way to manage old age
and the slowing down that goes with it

is to laugh your way through it.
Growing old and wearing out, experts assure us,

is a natural process, something human types share
with other animals and species.

Nothing remarkable about it, except in the way
some people look at it -

as they observe themselves from outside
and say with a smile and a shrug:

"That's not me, is it?"

Inventory

A meditation on Matthew Chapter 6, Verse 19
"Do not store up for yourselves treasures on earth"

By a kind of accounting which at first
seems highly unusual, nobody owns anything,
at least not for long –

not houses or acres of land
not a dog or a cat
and certainly not a friend or a spouse

The only things that can be kept
are offered to all,
cannot be weighed or measured

and never run down or wear out

Becoming Yourself

(a note to myself and others)

It doesn't usually happen

all at once

in a shining moment of revelation.

Mostly it arrives in bits and pieces.

But it's easier, by far,

and much more fun

to become who you are

than to try as hard as you can

to become who you aren't.

PART 3

Rounding Third
(From "Opening Doors")

Rounding Third

Baseball is an unusual sport.
Some find it boring.

Games have no time limit.
Unlike more fast- moving sports,
there are plenty of pauses.

Players often strike out.
One hit in three trips to the
plate is a very good average.

But there's something
about baseball
that speaks to the heart,

including the word home:
-home plate
-home run
-rounding third and heading for home.

Baseball is the only game
I know of where the goal is
to get back to where you started.

Botanical Wonder

In the middle of a botanical garden
filled with birds, bees, butterflies
and seasonal flowers of every
description, I came across

a large piece of petrified wood.
There it was,
right in front of me,
something reputed to be
90 million years old
but looking in very good shape.

It was a real tree when
dinosaurs were tramping around.
Then surviving in petrified form
when they disappeared.

I would like to have asked
some questions of this ancient specimen
of a tree:

-When did those dinosaurs disappear?
-Did cats and dogs show up soon after that?
-When did humans first appear?

I wished that stony tree could
give me a half hour to tell its
story in an abbreviated way.

It didn't seem unapproachable
and the time would have passed
very quickly.

Fitting In

Nobody wants to be considered

-a square peg in a round hole
-a fifth wheel
-or, God forbid, a misfit.

It's not a bad thing
To want to fit in
To a group or society
Of which there are
Many varieties.

But the kind of belonging
To which I mostly aspire
Is one where none are excluded:
No ins or outs
No one higher or lower

Where all that's required
Is to find the space
That's waiting for you
And then
Try to fill it

Resolutions

Resolution # 1

Slowly,
Over the years,
I've learned that
If you have nothing to say,
Don't say it.
Don't pretend
That you do.
Today
I have nothing to say
So I'll try
Not to say it.

Resolution # 2

Just look.
Be aware
Of what's around you,
How you might
Fit into the picture,
What you might do
Or not do,
Say or not say.
Then say it
Or do it.

"I Don't Know"

These words,
carved into a piece of wood,
made me smile.
I found the honesty refreshing.

Seems to be no shortage
of answer people,
quick to declare how to

- fix the economy
-make money
-improve your marriage
-lose weight
-get right with God

No time for questions.
No room for doubt.
No place for mystery.

Makes you want to go out
and get some fresh air.

Saying "I don't know"
might make it possible

to learn something
you didn't know before.

Gifts Given

This isn't a Christmas or a
birthday poem, or one about
occasions when, for whatever
reason, people give
or receive gifts.

It's simply a confession
that there are moments
when I become aware
of gifts that have been given,
some a long time ago.

Such moments can't be programmed
or written into a calendar.
They resist regimentation
and just appear,
welcomed but not planned for.

The gift of support, freely offered.
Unexpected kindnesses
from friends and strangers.
A wise word, nearly forgotten,
all of a sudden making sense.

There they are, these unplanned gifts,
like the bright red leaves
of a red maple tree
across the valley
on a clear September day.

Finding Your Voice

Unless they have laryngitis,
it doesn't seem to be a problem
for animals to find their voice. It's
natural for a dog to bark and
for birds to sing the songs
allotted to their species.

For us humans finding your voice
is a different thing.
It's more a matter of saying
what you want to say,
conveying to others
what you wish to convey.

Some find their voice in fixing
broken things, like cars and lawnmowers.
Some in writing, painting, cooking,
helping the neighbors
or making people laugh.

There are things inside us
yearning to emerge
and order any obstacles to
get out of the way.

What's Wrong With Goats?

How did goats get such a bad rap, as
in "separate the sheep from the goats"
with the goats losing out
in the last judgment?

But why? What did they do
to offend the judge?
Is it because sheep are docile
and goats stubborn

or eat with less discrimination?
Must be some history
to this goat prejudice.
People talk about scapegoats.
Never heard of a scapesheep.
It isn't even a word.

Running Out

One of the things
folks worry about
is running out,
as in running out of money
at the end of the month

or running out of time
to meet a deadline
or that one's health
could easily decline.

Is that why we rush around,
trying to capture whatever it is
that eludes us?

Have we missed springs
coming out of the
ground, bread provided
day after day,
as much as we need,

reminding us
the world is full of
renewable things?

One Raspberry

On July 5 of this year
I walked down to the raspberry patch
To check on the berries
As I do most days this time of the year
To try to discover when those berries
Would be ready to pick.

There they were,
Thousands of berries, I think,
Though it's anyone's guess.
Yet not one that I could see
Ripe enough to eat.
Not until I came upon, at the end of my tour,

One almost ripe raspberry
Which could be eatable the very next day.
It seemed as though this lone ripe raspberry
Was sending a message which went
Something like this: "Try to be mellow
You impatient man

If you possibly can.
In a week or two there will be so many of us
You won't know what to do with us.
Plenty for cereal or pie or jam.
Enough to give to the neighbors.
By the end of this month or early the next

You might get sick of us."

Fishing Expedition

Went fishing today.

Tried to catch a poem,

Hoping to pull one

Out of the water

But none were biting.

All I caught was

A couple of platitudes.

They weren't worth much

So I threw them back in.

November Beauty

A little starker,
a little plainer
than the month before it
or the month after.

Fields turning brown,
color fading,
if not already gone.
No more leaf tours
or chicken pie suppers
for north country visitors.

November is what it is,
a prelude to winter.
It ends with a holiday,
the least commercial,
most inclusive of any,
called simply Thanksgiving.

Washing The Dishes

There's something therapeutic
about washing the dishes.
after eating a supper
cooked by my spouse.

I like to wipe off the counters,
rinse off the plates
and load up the dishwasher
while shifting my mind into neutral.

You can think of anything
or nothing at all. I might or might
not wonder about the weather
while scrubbing a pan.

This activity connects me to my
father who used to wash dishes
without help from a dishwasher.
I feel part of a succession of people.

In a world that's uncertain
dishwashing is a tangible thing.
Take a look at that counter, I say
to myself. It looks a lot better.

Emptying The Trash

It's my duty and privilege
to gather the trash
at least two times a week.

Doesn't call for much thought.
It has a certain rhythm
as I empty the wastebaskets
into a large black plastic bag
which goes into a container
in the shed.

Sometimes, when proceeding
through this ritual,
I whistle or sing
a little off key

wishing it were as easy
to dump out
those useless odds and ends
That rattle around
in my head.

For My Mother

My mother died at age sixty-two,
when I was almost twenty- three.
Recently, while doing some housecleaning,
my wife discovered a picture of her,
a twenty-five year old bride
carrying a bouquet of lilies of the valley.

Who could have guessed that pretty
young woman had such a well of wisdom
and humor and love within her?

Who, looking at this picture,
would have known how forgiving
she would turn out to be to the last of her
five children, her late blooming son, tied up
in his own little world, not yet
able to give back the kind of
love she so consistently offered?

Yet somehow I feel sure she would have
both forgiven and truly forgotten any
worry or pain I had caused her.
The bride in this picture,
grown older, her hair almost white,
seemed to have cancelled my debts
in advance and would wonder
what on earth I was talking about.

Believing

According to some who've
Thought about the matter
The opposite of faith is not doubt.
It's certainty.

If all questions of life and death
Can be wrapped up
In a container
What room remains for mystery?
Or anything that doesn't fit?

To declare doubt and faith opposites
Is like saying winter and spring have
No connection,
And what you can't see isn't there.
But faith, according to one scripture
Writer, is evidence of things
Unseen.

No airtight case for God
Provable in a court of law
Has been provided.
Only stories
Of lost people found,
Homecomings
And broken things mended.

Weighty Matters

(With apologies to Meister Eckhart 1260-1327)

According to a man named
Meister Eckhart, the key to
a happier life
is in learning to let things go -

Like not staying angry at so and so
even if you think he or she is
a so and so,
or looking down at somebody else,
or trying to get even.

Learn to let go, Meister Eckhart
might say. Don't hold on to that
stuff. It's not what you've added
that makes you feel lighter.
It's what you've subtracted.

Assisted Living

As used now, "assisted living" is
a technical term applied to
people who need help getting through
the day and who, without such
assistance, might become confused
and, in some cases, wander away not
knowing where they were going.

Might that be too restrictive a definition?
Who among us knows exactly
where she or he is heading and needs
no assistance in finding their way?
No parent, no mentor, no teacher, no
doctor, no friend, no elder, no listener?
No one to stand by and cheer, or perhaps
tell you to wait a minute or give you a
kick in the rear?

I can't imagine anyone of any age
not needing assistance. What nonsense!
What foolishness even to think you
can go it alone! So thanks to all the
assisters who have become a part of my
life – my parents, my children, my wife-
and to X, Y and Z, among
others. Too many to count.

Sabbaths

A Sabbath, whatever the day or the hour,
Is time set apart
To be reminded
Of things forgotten
Or never known.

Time to picture a way of living
Where the first
Shall be last and
The meek
Inherit the earth.

Time to see through illusions
Of money and power
And laugh at pretenses,
Both our own
And others.

To view with new eyes
The world around and within.
Time to remember
The One who made us.

Observing a Sabbath
Turns the tables on everything.

PART 4

Common Property
(From "Connected")

Common Property

I wonder if there is such a thing
as an original idea, one that
nobody ever thought of before?

I'm inclined toward the opinion
that there isn't
and that the good ones are common

property - not patented or copyrighted.
Nobody owns them.
So anybody who wants to

can pull one out of the air
and recycle it - including the idea
that if you win so do I

and if you lose I do too
for the simple reason that,
as different as we may be,

you're connected to me
and I'm connected to you.

Pretending

It's hard work to pretend,
to try to be what you're not.
Goes against the grain -

as in forcing a smile,
holding back tears,
trying to look serious
when you can hardly keep
a straight face.

Other animals don't seem
to have this pretending problem.
They are what they are.

It's taken me a long time
to begin to discover
that the best thing a person
can become

is what, deep down
he or she already is.

Walking

Our neighbor, Rith,
Is very faithful
About bundling up
These cold winter days

And circling around
The quadrangle connecting
Six of the cottages
In Hartmeadow Village

Pushing her walker
Ahead of her
Three or four times
Around the circle.

She does it without
Fanfare, simply
Putting one foot
In front of the other

Observing An Ant

Noticed an ant this morning,
a garden-variety black ant
walking purposefully along
the bathroom floor.

This ant was carrying an object.
I couldn't tell what it was,
except that it was as big
as the ant.

I had no appetite for stepping
on this ant
which seemed so dedicated
and gainfully employed.

As it headed this way and that
running into one barrier after another
I felt a bond to the ant,
hoping it would find its way

to wherever it wanted to go.
Even thought I'd try to pick it up
and take it outside but it
disappeared under a radiator.

A Fly On The Wall

Have you ever wanted to be
a fly on the wall,
listening in on conversations
when nobody knows you're there?

That thought is quite appealing to me.
You could visit a gathering
of most any sort

and, if it becomes boring,
fly away to another location
without causing a commotion.

As an experienced fly on the wall
you could describe your adventures,
including the testimonial dinner

when a waiter spotted you there
and took a swipe at you with
a flyswatter, but missed.

Northern Robins

When I looked out the window
on a very cold January morning,
I saw a whole flock of robins
in our back yard – sixty or more of them.

They were large, healthy looking robins
who looked like they'd dropped by
for a snack.

You had to laugh as you watched them
waddling around the yard,
their bellies almost touching the ground.

They're called Canadian Robins,
a friend explained,
not the kind you see in the summer
pulling up worms on the lawn.

These robins like berries and,
one would guess, whatever they found
in our back yard.

Good for these robins, I thought,
showing up on one of the coldest
days in the year,

not so much as a sign of spring
but as an example of how to
get through the winter.

Northern Spring

It's here again
In New England.

It arrived
Just when you thought

It never would.
Sooner or later

It shows up,
Greeting the world

In various shades
Of green, red and yellow,

Reminding us,
When we feared

It was gone for good,
That it was only hiding.

Smitten

How can you fall in love
with a vegetable garden?
That seems like an odd thing to do
to put it mildly.

A row of beans is not especially
romantic and those feathery
carrot plants are not at all
dramatic.

Hardly anyone would consider
a squash vine as sexy
and that row of beets, featuring
wide gaps between plants,
is an embarrassment.

But, taken together,
there's something appealing
about a vegetable garden -
an attraction hard to explain.
So I won't try.

Holy Cows

One of the nice things
about living in North Danville, Vermont
part of the year
is seeing so many cows.

We pass them on the way
into or out of town.
Sometimes they're standing up,
sometimes lying down.

On certain occasions
we need to stop the car
and wait while they cross the road,
either going out to the field

or back to the barn.
They're lovable creatures.
Can't imagine them hurting a soul
unless one of them stumbled
and fell on somebody.

Cows just do what they do –
eat, give milk, chew their cuds,
while sending calming vibrations
into the atmosphere.

Can't say the same for bulls
but this is a poem about cows.

Disorderly Abundance

There's no name for this season
in the life of a garden.
It arrives, more or less,
in the second half of August.
Now here it is again!

I failed to provide the tomato plants
enough support and they're
mingling with the cucumbers,
which are infringing on the territory
of the beans.

Another row of beans is covering up
the onions
and the squash is overshadowing
some nearby carrots.
The garden has become a disorganized mess
but a productive one.

The trouble with this cascade of food
is that it doesn't last.
You can only eat so much squash
or swiss chard.

So it's a matter of passing on what you can
before it spoils.
It's time to pick some more beans!

Hard Working Neighbor

Among our neighbors
at Hartmeadow Village
is a beaver who can,
if he or she wishes,
swim through a culvert

while going from one
side of the road to the other,
commuting to work – that
work being cutting down trees
with its remarkable
front teeth.

Beavers have no questions
as to their vocation.
They just set about doing what
nature assigned them to do -

creating beaver dams
where water gathers,
forming a beaver pond.
Their equally remarkable tails
make them good swimmers too.

Candle Lighting

It's mostly symbolic.
Plain old light bulbs do better
At illuminating
The space around them.

Yet lighting candles is a practice
That shows no signs
Of going out of business.

People light them for
All kinds of occasions-

celebrating a birthday,
remembering a friend,
protesting a killing,
giving thanks for food

It's kind of ceremonial
And doesn't accomplish much
You can see.

But we human types
Need rituals and ceremonies
Almost as much as water and air

And to declare in no uncertain terms
That things not seen are still there.

A Drink Of Water

No other drink can quite compare
to a pure, cold glass of water.
H2O isn't an exciting beverage.
It's not sweet. It's not sour.

It lacks the vitamins of
orange juice, mangos
or tomatoes.

Nor can it be compared
to beer, wine or Scotch,
let alone coffee or tea.

If not chlorinated or otherwise
doctored,
it has no flavor at all.

How can such a bland beverage
be so refreshing and satisfying,
as thirsty people of all times and places
have claimed it to be?

About Hearing

(for the semi deaf)

When you're classified
as hard of hearing
some questions arise,

among them...

What aren't you hearing?
What matters of substance,
pieces of information
and gossip
are you missing?

Is it possible to hear and
not hear at the same time,
not getting the words but
sensing the meaning?

Whatever the case it
would be a good thing
to hear the words clearly, thereby
avoiding answering questions

people aren't asking.

True Believing

A new strain of an old disease
has recently been discovered
in the United States.
Call it True Believer – itis.

It's not the first time this affliction
has appeared on our soil.
Most likely,
won't be the last.

The symptoms of
the latest outbreak include

a fear if losing what you have
followed by a refusal to compromise

To keep True Believer-itis from spreading
the following remedies
may be of help –

a dose of humility and
an application of common sense

It seems like those who get it right
most of the time
are the ones who admit
they might be wrong.

Old Men Cry Easily

Some old men cry easily

-at arrivals
-at departures
-on any occasion at all

It's downright disgusting!
Sentimental old fools!

What in the world is the matter with them?
Are they coming apart at the seams?
Has some part of their brain
Become disconnected
From the rest of it?

Or could they be finally getting
Some sense in their heads

As they begin to realize that life is
A mixture of laughter and tears

And no one is telling them anymore
That boys don't cry?

An Observation

Some poems disappoint you.
They start out looking promising

as though, guided by an unerring
instinct, they know where they're going

and how to get there.
But then, to your surprise,

they begin to wander
this way and that

and then suddenly collapse
in a rush of stale air.

Pursuing Happiness

Happiness can't be pursued directly.

It's too elusive, we are told.

But that doesn't mean it can't

just show up,

catching up with you

from time to time.

Requiem For A Rototiller

I suppose it could be fixed
and made to last a little longer,
tilling the soil in the vegetable garden,

something it's done for the last eighteen years-
until the end of last season
when it wouldn't start.

It didn't cost a lot.
Doesn't owe me anything.
But it's been satisfying

to see it mixing maple leaves
and cow manure into the soil,
making the ground a more hospitable space

for vegetables to grow.
A word of appreciation
doesn't seem out of place.

Where To Look

I've decided that I belong to
That class of people
Who believe all good things
Come from nearby,
Within easy reach.
Not from a distant location
Or lofty proclamation.

But from seeds scattered
On the ground,
Like ideas making their way
To the surface,
Emerging from below.

In good soil these seeds grow.
How that happens is a mystery.
They just do,
Appearing in the humblest of guises
Like the face of a child,
The smile of a stranger,
The shade of a tree.

All at once there they are,
Shaking foundations,
Upsetting calculations,
Turning right-side up
What was upside down.

Glue

(To whom it may concern)

There are many types of glue
which can be
bought at the store
and used around the house.

No need to list them here.
What they all have in common
is the ability to hold things together,
like the parts of a chair.

Glue is not something
which calls attention to itself.
It functions best when not seen –
shoring up shaky places
and filling empty spaces,

as do some people
who have a way of holding together

a family
a team
whatever.

It doesn't seem like a compliment
to compare persons to glue,
but it makes sense because
you can't help but notice
if they're not there.

Elusive

What in the world is a soul?
Is it what makes you, you and me, me?

Souls can't be weighed, measured
Or pinned down on a chart
Like a butterfly in a biology lab.

Souls are elusive.
There's a wildness about them
That resists captivity.

But sometimes you can spot them
As you listen to a pianist play the piano
Or observe people helping each other

During hard times.
Souls are who we are and
Who we are meant to be.

When somebody dies it's obvious
That what was there
Isn't there anymore.

What happened to it?
Where did it go?
Did it evaporate into space?

Or is it still present,
As elusive as ever,
In a wider place?

Other books by Van Parker:

"Opening Doors"
"Connected"